FUTURE SPACE

BEYOND EARTH

Author: David Jefferis
Illustrator: Sebastian Quigley
Consultant: Mat Irvine, FBIS

Created and produced by Firecrest Books Ltd
in association with Alpha Communications and
Sebastian Quigley/Linden Artists

Copyright © 2001 Firecrest Books Ltd,
Alpha Communications, and
Sebastian Quigley/Linden Artists

Scholastic and Tangerine Press™ and associated logos are trademarks of Scholastic Inc

Published by Tangerine Press™, an imprint of Scholastic Inc;
555 Broadway; New York, NY 10012

10 9 8 7 6 5 4 3 2 1

ISBN 0-439-31460-7

Printed and bound in Italy
First Printing September 2001

FUTURE SPACE
BEYOND EARTH

David Jefferis
Consultant **Mat Irvine, FBIS**
Illustrated by **Sebastian Quigley**

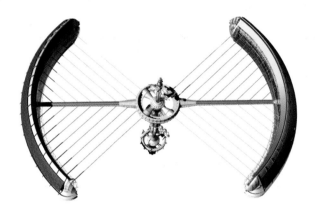

Tangerine Press™ and associated logo and
design are trademarks of Scholastic Inc.

Consultant
Mat Irvine, FBIS

Publishing Consultant
Peter Sackett

Designer and Art Director
Phil Jacobs

Editor
Norman Barrett

Extra artwork by
Roger Stewart/Virgil Pomfret Artists and Phil Jacobs

Project Coordinator
Pat Jacobs

Color separation in England by
CK Digital

Printed in Italy by
Grafica Editoriale Printing

CONTENTS

SPACE STATIONS

The idea of a space station – a human outpost on the high frontier – is not new. Science-fiction writers led the way many years ago with stories that featured fantastic wheel-shaped structures. But the reality started off more modestly in the 1970s – a series of single-module Russian Salyuts and the U.S. Skylab, which was made from an empty Saturn rocket fuel-tank! The bigger Russian Mir (Peace) space station stayed in orbit for 15 years, until 2001. But now a giant is being built in space – it's a football field sized flying laboratory called the International Space Station. Parts for the space station (also known as ISS or Alpha) are transported by U.S. Space Shuttles and Russian rockets.

Experiments in space

So what is the point of the ISS? It's certainly not a space hotel, even though it had a tourist visit for a week in 2001. Its real job is to be a huge research laboratory, testing many things that are of immediate importance to the well-being of the Earth and the future of mankind – as well as others that are valuable to the advancement of science.

For example, experiments have been designed to find ways to use energy more efficiently and to improve the quality of air and water. These are vital to people living on the ISS, but will also make life better here on Earth. Earth observers on the ISS will check on the state of our world. And astronomers will be able to look deeper and deeper into space to discover more secrets of the universe.

Russia's 130-ton Mir station was directed back to Earth in 2001. It broke up in the atmosphere and crashed in the ocean.

Skylab (1973) was a U.S. space station made by fitting a rocket fuel-tank with built-in living equipment.

The ISS should look like this when completed. There will be a crew of up to seven at any one time.

Astronaut uses special screwdriver to tighten bolts in new structure being added to ISS.

Backpack contains air supply, plus heating and cooling systems. Astronaut can take spacewalk lasting several hours.

This long truss is the lightweight "backbone" of the ISS.

ISLAND IN THE SKY

Facts and figures behind the ISS show it to be a colossal project. As planned, the finished station will be the biggest human-made object ever built in space, measuring 356 feet (108.5 m) by 290 feet (88.4 m). The ISS will be a massive object, too – on Earth it would weigh around 450 tons. Inside there will be about the same amount of room as in a big airplane, though much of this will be given over to machinery and science experiments. On early missions there are just three astronauts aboard at the same time, but eventually the ISS will be home for a crew of up to seven.

Building a space station

Putting together such a large structure is not something that can be done all at once. The ISS is made of a number of parts, or modules, which clip together in space, much like the parts of a giant-size model kit. Among these is the Russian-built Zarya (Sunrise) control module. This was the first part of the ISS to be launched (November 1998). Zarya has engines on board for adjusting the ISS orbiting height and position in space. It also has docking ports, so that supply craft can latch on with fresh food, air, and other vital supplies and equipment brought from Earth.

The ISS is not far away from our planet. It orbits at a height of only about 220 miles (350 km). If you could travel by automobile, the trip straight up would take less than 4 hours at highway speeds.

Solar cell "wings" provide power in space. They convert the energy in sunlight to electricity, which is needed to keep the complex systems aboard ISS working properly.

Sixteen countries are involved in the ISS, including Japan, which is making this research module called Kibo (Hope), due to be launched in 2004.

The modules that make up the ISS have to be produced very precisely so that they fit together perfectly when joined in orbit.

Solar cell wings provide power for the ISS.

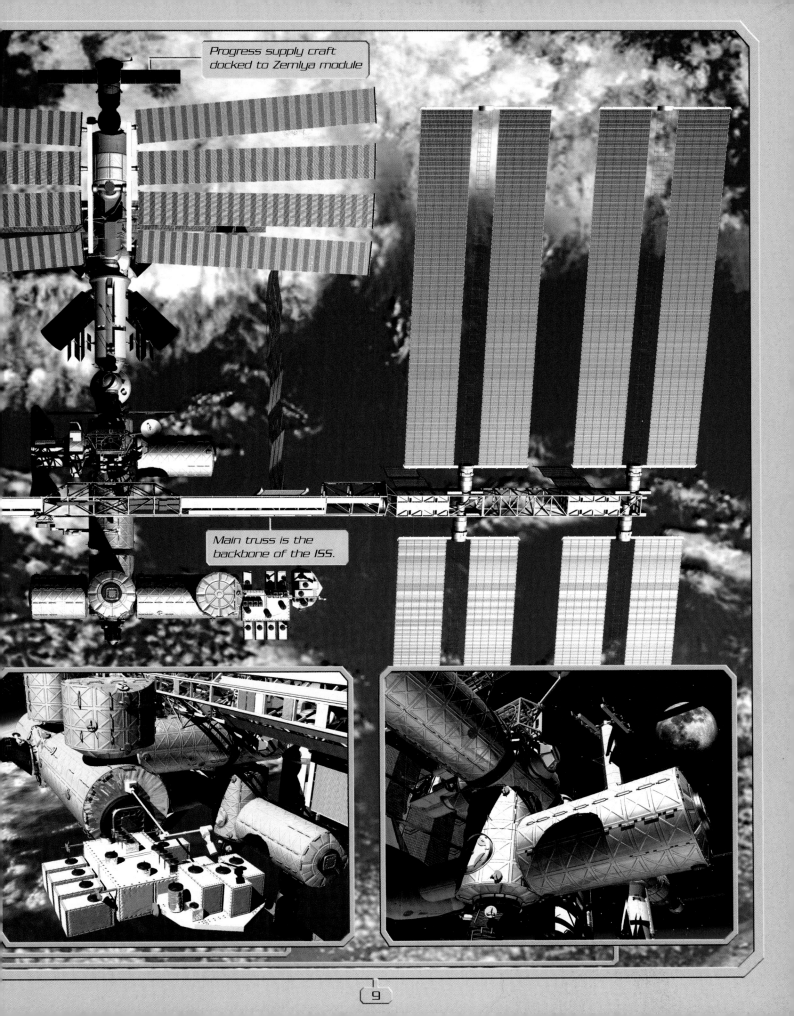

Progress supply craft docked to Zemlya module

Main truss is the backbone of the ISS.

SPACE WALKERS

When the first space stations were sent into orbit, they were small enough to be launched as complete units. But the ISS is too big to be launched all at once. Most of the construction has to be done in space. Much of this can be completed with the aid of the remote-control manipulator arm or with free-flying robot craft. But there will always be times where an astronaut has to put on a spacesuit and venture into space.

Spacesuits have been improved over the years, but they are still bulky. Care is vital – for space is a deadly environment. A suit is a "mini-spacecraft," and without its oxygen supply and heating and cooling systems an astronaut would last no more than a few minutes. The astronauts are connected by tethers to the main structure of the ISS. And there are grab handles spaced around the modules for pulling themselves carefully around.

Working in space

Space-walking, or Extra-Vehicular Activity (EVA), as it is officially called, gives an amazing feeling of freedom. But safety is vital – hence the tether lines. For tasks further away than lines will stretch or for more freedom of movement, astronauts wear a manned maneuvering unit (MMU). This is propelled by small gas jets and worn like an oversized spacesuit backpack.

Exit from the space station is through an "airlock." You enter, seal the door shut, and wait for the air to be pumped out. Then the outer door swings open.

Many ISS construction tasks can be performed with the Canadian-made robot manipulator arm (the Canadarm), a bigger version of the Shuttle's arm.

Two astronauts practice space-assembly in a water tank on Earth. Floating in the water is rather like floating in space. Divers are on hand to help if needed.

An approachi[ng] Space Shuttle

The remote-control Canadarm 2 is used to move large sections into place.

Grab handles are positioned all over the ISS.

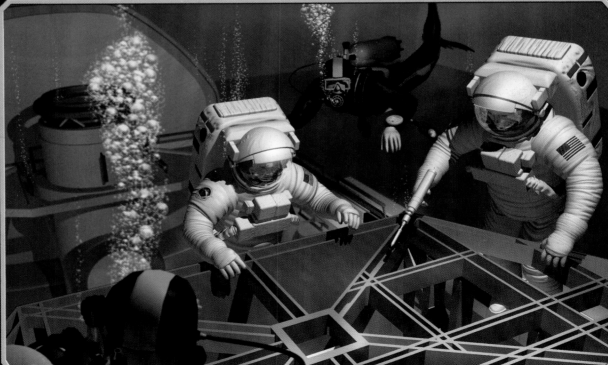

LINKUP IN SPACE

The U.S. Space Shuttle will be the main transportation to the ISS for many years. It takes crews to and from the station, and brings cargo and many of the modules and other structures needed for building the ISS to its full size. Astronauts and supplies are also brought by the Russians, with crewed Soyuz and uncrewed Progress craft.

A Space Shuttle Orbiter flies in space with its cargo bay doors open. The doors contain radiators to get rid of the intense heat generated by the direct rays from the Sun. Shuttles that dock with the ISS have a docking adapter in the forward end of the cargo bay, but there is still plenty of space available for carrying cargo.

Delivery trucks

As the ISS grows, more and more supplies will be needed. Three Multi-Purpose Logistic Modules (MPLMs) have been built to ferry delicate equipment and provisions. These are the "delivery trucks" of the ISS and can each carry up to 9 tons of supplies. An MPLM travels in the cargo bay of the Shuttle and is then docked with the ISS. The crew crawls through the docking hatch to move the stores into the station. The MPLM is then undocked and placed back into the Shuttle cargo bay for return to Earth. The MPLMs are made by the Italian Space Agency and are named after famous Italian artists of the past – Leonardo, Donatello, and Raffaello (Raphael).

A Shuttle Orbiter approaches the ISS. The bay doors are open so their radiators can discharge the heat from the Sun. The Orbiter carries a new module for the Space Station.

One of the MPLMs is unloaded from the Shuttle cargo bay by the remote arm. It will be docked with the main station while its supplies are moved.

New unmanned craft are being developed by several space agencies to take supplies to the ISS.

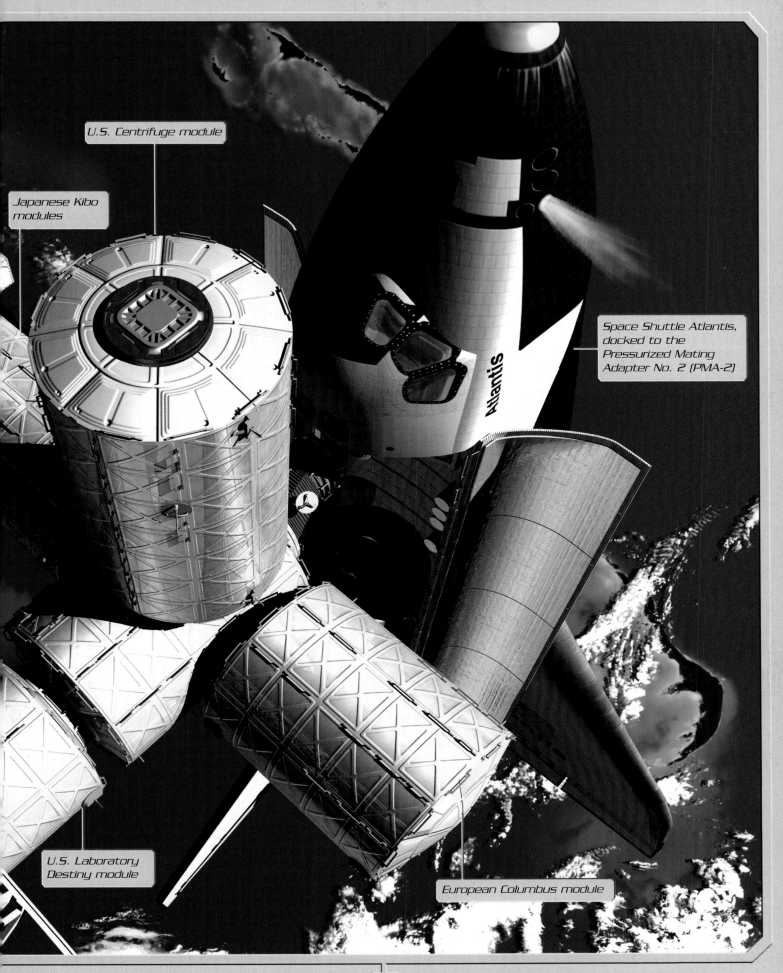

U.S. Centrifuge module

Japanese Kibo modules

Space Shuttle Atlantis, docked to the Pressurized Mating Adapter No. 2 (PMA-2)

U.S. Laboratory Destiny module

European Columbus module

Atlantis

LIVING IN ORBIT

Living in space is very different than living in a normal house on Earth. But some activities are similar, as astronauts also eat, sleep, and wash up. But don't expect to be able to take a bath – ISS crews have to have showers in an enclosed cubicle, using only a small amount of treated, recycled water. A special toilet has also been developed for the ISS – it has a lot of plumbing and a vacuum pump to suck the waste away. Food is mostly pre-prepared, and the crew uses a microwave oven to heat it. Any leftovers have to be squashed down carefully and sealed in bags. Great care must be taken not to let the tiniest crumb escape, as it would float around and might get into delicate equipment.

Exercise and relaxation

Exercise on the ISS is essential. Without gravity, muscles weaken, and bones become brittle, so special machines have been developed to help astronauts keep in shape.

One big advantage that ISS crews do have is that the usable space is greater than its equivalent on Earth. Being able to float around means that a "ceiling" can be just as useful as a "floor." And ISS crews have another special bonus not found back home – an amazing view through portholes of our blue planet passing below. Then, after a day's work, they have sleeping bags that can be hung up virtually anywhere.

ISS crew have relaxation time so they can take advantage of – and maybe photograph – the view of the Earth below.

Daily exercise in space is very important, and special "treadmills" – walking machines – have been developed for use in orbit.

Being able to float aboard a space station means you can use all six surfaces as "walls" – but you have to be careful tools and equipment don't float away from you!

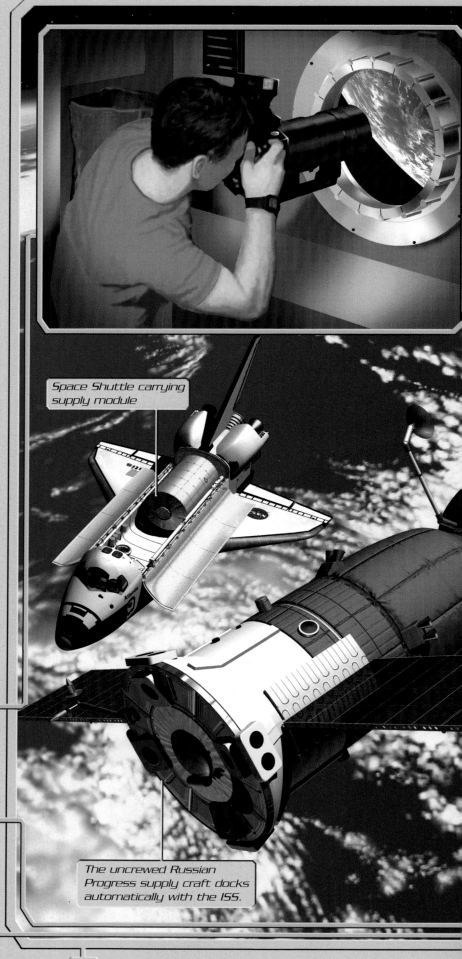

Space Shuttle carrying supply module

The uncrewed Russian Progress supply craft docks automatically with the ISS.

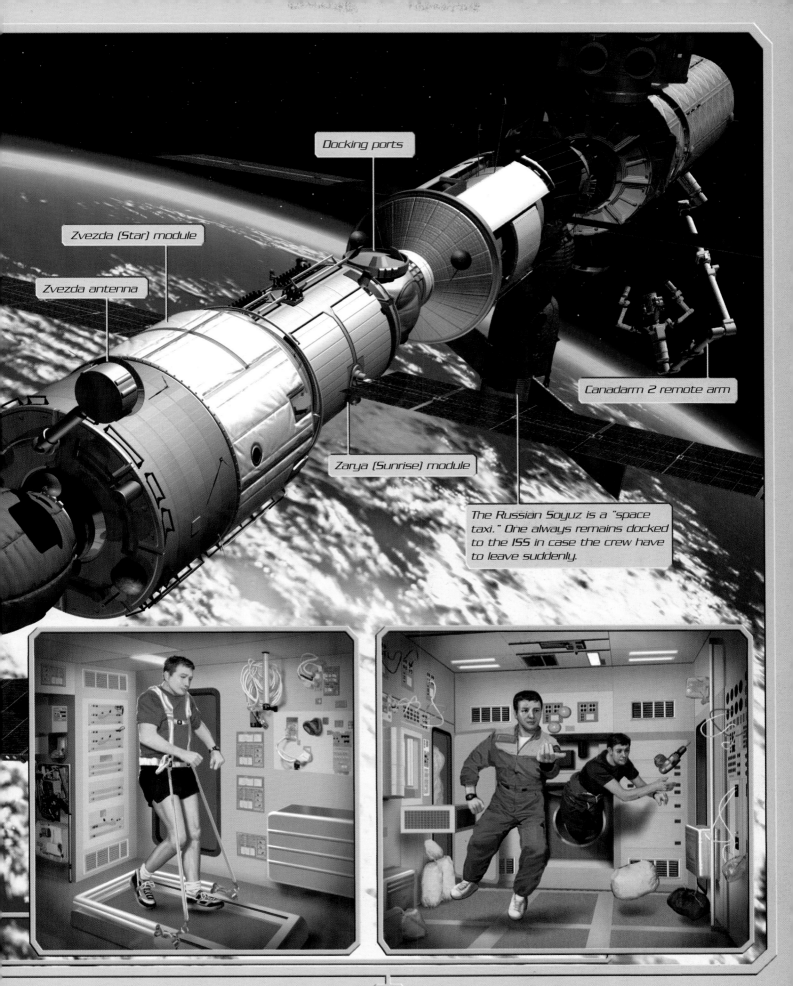

Docking ports

Zvezda (Star) module

Zvezda antenna

Zarya (Sunrise) module

Canadarm 2 remote arm

The Russian Soyuz is a "space taxi." One always remains docked to the ISS in case the crew have to leave suddenly.

INTERNATIONAL OBSERVER

The ISS travels around the Earth at about 17,500 mph (28,000 km/h). As a result, it takes only about 80 minutes for the ISS to pass completely around the Earth. So science instruments and astronaut-scientists get a grand, 360-degree view of our planet. Off-duty astronauts spend a lot of time gazing through the portholes, as did Dennis Tito, the world's first "space tourist." A U.S. citizen who paid for his flight, Tito took dozens of pictures with his own camera. The ISS is indeed a "window on the world."

Viewing the Earth

Scientific photography is one of the top ways of checking out the health of our world. The ISS is moving in an orbit that allows instruments to view about three-quarters of the Earth's surface. And it is designed to observe for at least 15 years.

The crew of the ISS will be able to monitor and measure changes in such fields as pollution, weather patterns, and temperature with accuracy and consistency. This kind of information will enable scientists to investigate and warn of global warming or increases in pollution levels that might seriously affect life on Earth.

Many other people and organizations will also benefit from such data. It could help farmers and fishermen, for example, in planning food production.

Storm warnings are already much more efficent using satellite information. ISS research may help explain why such storms appear in the first place.

Special instruments can monitor the health of land and water areas, checking on such factors as surface temperature and pollution levels.

Problems in the atmosphere can be tracked from the ISS. Here are two views of Antarctica, showing the changes in size of the ozone hole.

View of a hurricane from space. This one is tracking toward the U.S. east coast.

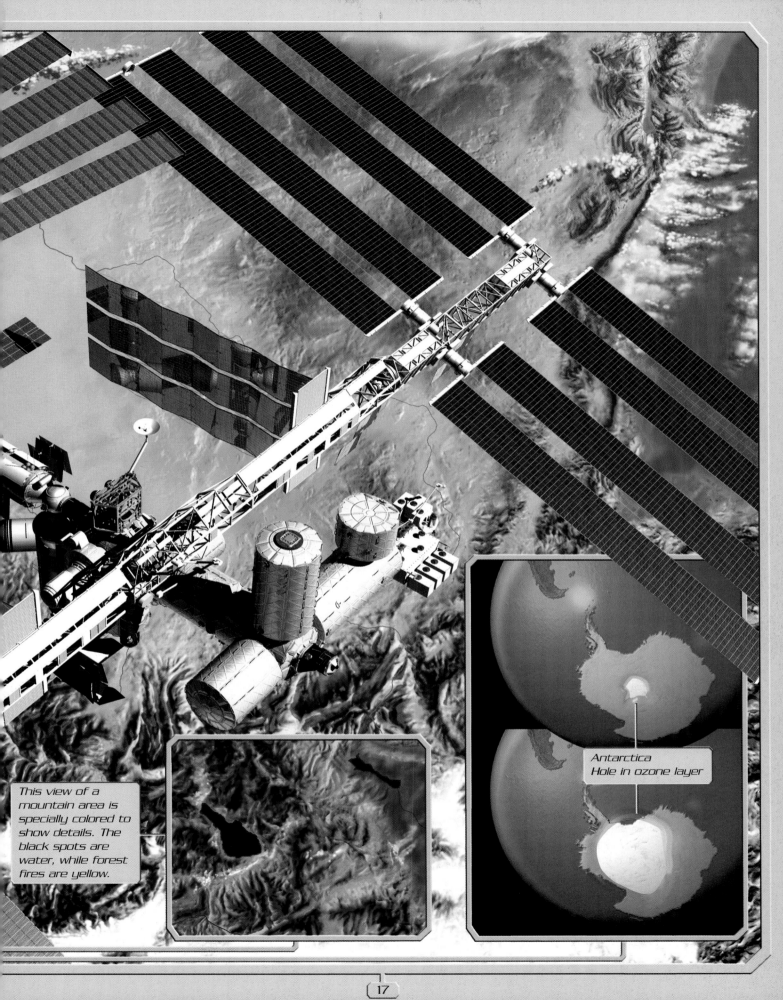

This view of a mountain area is specially colored to show details. The black spots are water, while forest fires are yellow.

Antarctica
Hole in ozone layer

SCIENCE FRONTIERS

Another important mission for ISS crews will be to investigate the space environment fully. Studying the Sun, checking out space "weather," and looking at stars and planets are all ISS tasks. As with the Earth experiments, researchers will be able to find out how things change over time.

But why bother using the ISS? Why not do research from the ground? The main reason is that space-based instruments are above the atmosphere, which is full of obscuring dust, vapor, and pollution. In space, a telescope has a crystal-clear view of the universe.

Many scientists question the need for human operators. It's true that many instruments can be remotely operated, but some experiments need a human to check progress.

Robot astronomers

Space telescopes themselves are not new. One of the most important is still the Hubble Space Telescope (HST), a truck-size satellite launched in 1990. The HST has solar cells for power and a large telescope in its central tube section. It is controlled from the ground, but a Space Shuttle visits every few years for repairs and to install new equipment.

The craft shown at right is one idea for a second-generation HST, equipped with high-tech instruments to see farther and clearer into space. It will float some distance from the ISS, and repairs could be carried out by a space-station team.

The HST was named after the U.S. scientist Edwin Hubble, a leading astronomer of the 1900s. The HST can point accurately at any object in space.

Space telescopes can spot very faint objects. Here a distant planet, bottom left, shows as a faint gleam next to its parent star.

New stars may be forming within these glowing gas clouds called the "Pillars of Creation." They are far away in deep space.

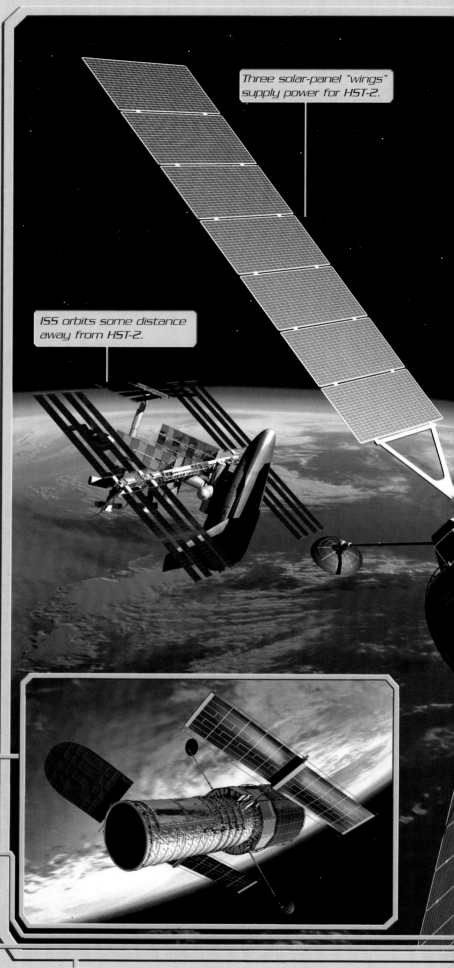

Three solar-panel "wings" supply power for HST-2.

ISS orbits some distance away from HST-2.

A target for HST-2 could be a black hole, seen here in an artist's rendition. Note that the black hole is invisible – what does show is the fierce storm of radiation that surrounds it.

HST-2 has a high-power telescope, designed to spot planets of other stars, known as "exo-planets."

EMERGENCY IN ORBIT

Despite the great care taken to reduce risks, all space flights are potentially dangerous. Earlier space stations have had their problems. One of these was when a Progress supply craft crashed into the Russian Mir station in 1997. Power on board was drastically reduced, and there was a danger the whole station would be lost. But the crew managed to make the necessary repairs in time, showing that a space accident need not be fatal.

Dangers in space

As well as crashes with supply craft, there is the danger of the ISS being hit by small chunks of space rock called "meteoroids." These hurtle through space at up to 45 miles per second (72 km/sec), and a pea size grain could have enough energy to puncture a wall. Other dangers include equipment on board malfunctioning. If the air supply fails, for example, the crew has only a limited time to fix things before it runs out.

In the event of an emergency, there will always be at least one rescue craft docked or nearby the ISS. In the early years of the ISS, the docked craft is normally the reliable Russian Soyuz, which will be regularly replaced with a new one to ensure the rescue vehicle is always in top condition.

A remote-control robot is used to repair a damaged solar panel. Such "helpers" save crew members from unnecessary spacewalks.

Future "space lifeboat" shuttlecraft like this one will be able to take ISS crew back to Earth.

An unmanned Progress craft crashed into the solar arrays of the Spektr module in 1997. This was a very serious incident, but no one was injured, and Mir was repaired. It lasted another four years.

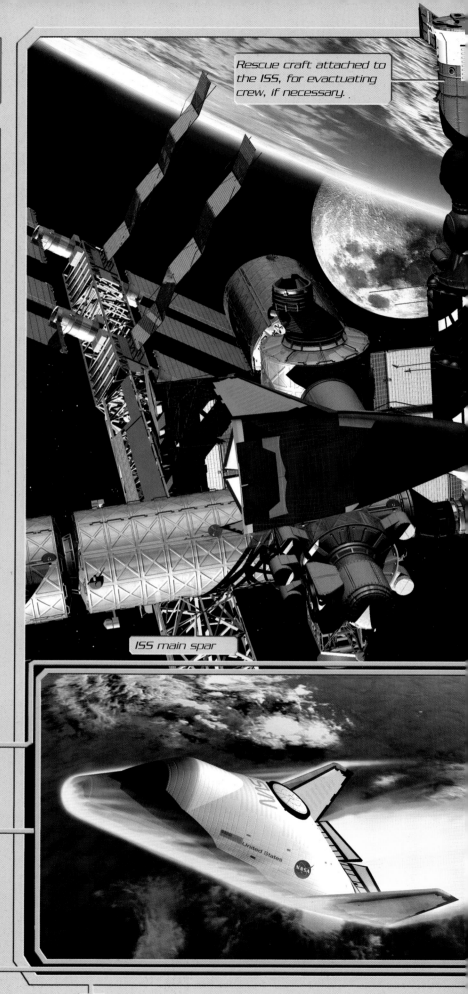

Rescue craft attached to the ISS, for evacuating crew, if necessary.

ISS main spar

SPACE MEDICINE

Medical research in space grabs few headlines, yet it is vital for future human exploration. Areas of research for ISS crews include finding out how and why our bones and muscles lose their strength without Earth's gravity pull. For future deep-space flights, answers to such problems, and cures for them, are essential. Other research looks at the effects of radiation on the body. On Earth we are protected quite well by our thick blanket of atmosphere. Even so, too much sunlight on unprotected skin can cause skin cancer. Beyond Earth, such radiation is many times more severe, and can kill cells, cause cancer, damage nerves, and much more.

Medical orbiter

The future medical orbiter shown here carries on the work begun by astronauts on the ISS. The color-coded pods at the rim are computerized mini-factories that make valuable drugs, using microgravity conditions to make them better and more easily than on Earth. The pods are removed regularly for delivery to Earth.

In the central spine, medical scientists carry out further research. Here there is also an emergency room to treat space workers. In the future there are likely to be many more people living and working in space, and so there will be occasional injuries or illnesses that need more care than a spacecraft's standard medical kit can provide. Doctors aboard the medical orbiter should be able to give the best treatment possible.

Regular medical checks in space are essential, including on the ISS. Here a medical-center doctor uses computer equipment to keep abreast of a space worker's health.

A "Phantom Torso" is carried on the ISS, and is about the same size and weight as an adult human. Its purpose is to measure how radiation affects our organs. Inside the torso are sensors placed in the same position as organs such as the brain, heart, lungs, and stomach.

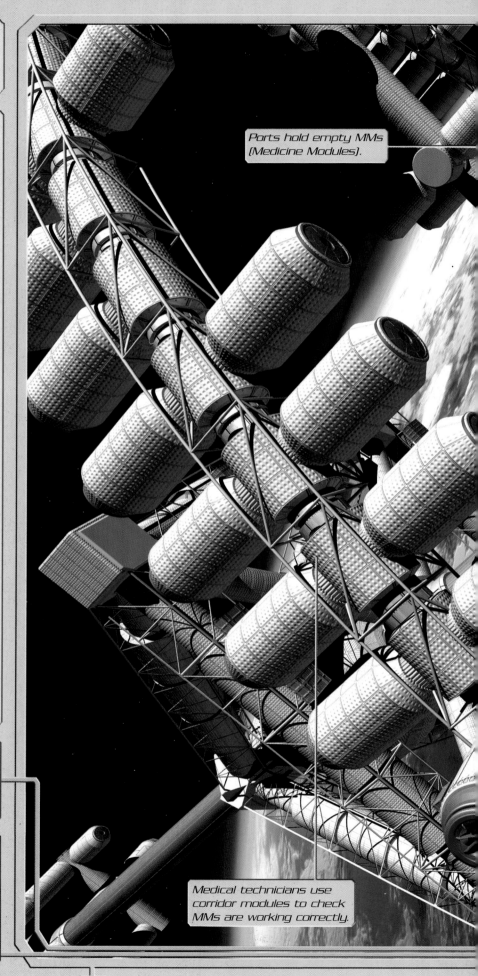

Ports hold empty MMs [Medicine Modules].

Medical technicians use corridor modules to check MMs are working correctly.

MMs are color-coded according to the type of product they are manufacturing.

Medical-center spine has areas for research, treatment, and long-term care.

SPACE TOURS

The main interest in space for many people is quite simple – "I want to go, so when can you take me?" Well, space vacations are not possible yet – at present space travel is really only for professional astronauts. Even so, several "guests" have already flown in orbit, including some journalists, and in 2001 American Dennis Tito paid millions of dollars for a special trip!

The space hotel

Space tourism may not be possible yet, but that doesn't stop people thinking of ways to make it so. The idea of an orbiting space hotel is popular, but size is the problem. One idea is to use discarded Space Shuttle fuel tanks. The external tank (ET) contains fuel for the Shuttle Orbiter engines on the way into orbit. But it is not recovered – when empty, it is allowed to fall back into the atmosphere and burn up. However, each ET has nearly 26,000 cubic feet (735 cubic meters) of room inside – more than an ample detached house. A group of ETs linked together could form the basis of the most exclusive hotel ever.

With more people going into space, a cheap, efficient way of getting them there will be needed. Eventually we may build craft that can take off and land at an airport, like airplanes of today. These "super-shuttles," or "spaceplanes," will probably look like sleek planes, but will be powered by rockets as well as jet engines.

A spaceplane arrives with a fresh set of tourists for the orbiting hotel.

A spaceplane takes off from an "aerospaceport" – destination, the world's first hotel in space. These super-shuttles will take off on jet power, then switch over to rockets for the climb into orbit.

One unique aspect of the shuttle-tank hotel will be the free-fall conditions of orbit. Here two guests get used to floating freely, while another tourist braves the outdoors in a spacesuit – always available for rent!

A Space Shuttle takes to the skies. The largest single part, the orange-colored external tank, is presently discarded after each launch.

ETs converted into hotel rooms

Tunnels connect ET living areas with the free-fall hub.

Free-fall area, where gravity is nearly zero

Solar arrays provide power.

Main hub

The hotel spins so that artificial gravity is generated at the outer edge – this means you won't float out of bed!

BATTLE STATION

Although various treaties on Earth currently forbid the use of space as a battleground, military satellites have been in place for many years. These include "spy" satellites that can view the Earth in remarkable detail from hundreds of miles in orbit. Some spy cameras can see the headlines on a newspaper!

Military planners are trying to build a missile shield in space (sometimes nicknamed Star Wars, after the movie) that can defend against an enemy missile attack. The idea is to locate, track, and destroy missiles either shortly after take-off or while they are climbing into orbit.

Many weapon concepts have also been dreamed up. One type uses very high-power laser beams to blind the enemy or even burn up enemy craft. Another uses "particle beams." These are intense beams of electronically charged particles, designed to disrupt the electronics of the incoming missiles.

Space bullets

The rail-gun fires a projectile by means of a magnetic track instead of the gunpowder of a conventional gun. This is known as a "kinetic-kill" weapon, firing "space bullets" that destroy enemy missiles with a knockout punch. But such Star Wars weapons need a huge amount of computing power to work properly, and many scientists think that they will never be totally successful.

Control of defense passes to computers as soon as the "fire" command key is turned – human reactions are too slow to hit fast moving objects in space consistently.

A rail-gun fires projectiles – "space bullets" – at the missiles, but would have to be extremely accurately aimed.

Laser beams could possibly be generated on Earth and aimed at satellites holding giant mirrors. These would reflect the beam at enemy missiles.

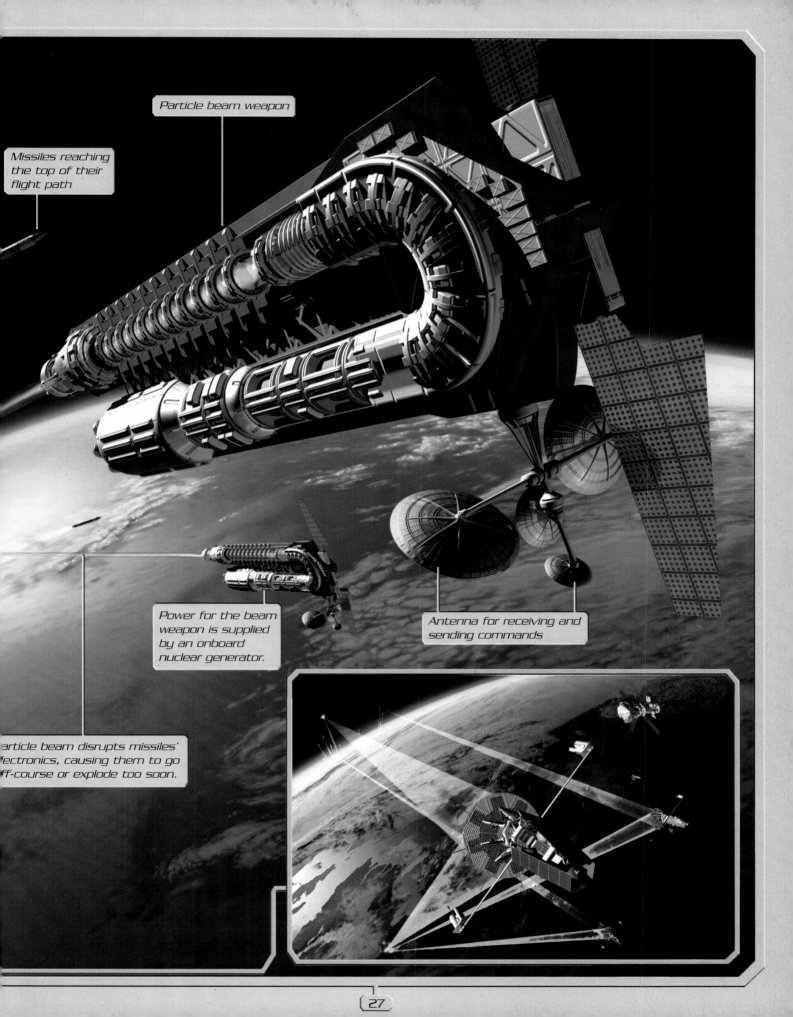

Particle beam weapon

Missiles reaching the top of their flight path

Power for the beam weapon is supplied by an onboard nuclear generator.

Antenna for receiving and sending commands

Particle beam disrupts missiles' electronics, causing them to go off-course or explode too soon.

SPACE FACTORY

At present, we can only guess at what the space factory of the future will make. But there are some obvious advantages in using space for making things. One is the near-weightless environment – it's actually called "microgravity," about one-billionth of the gravity pull we feel on Earth. A manufacturing process that we know benefits from this is growing crystals. Crystals grow much larger in microgravity. Another material to profit from microgravity is foamed metal. If bubbles of gas are introduced into molten metals, the metals remain just as strong, but are much lighter. On Earth, the bubbles rise to the surface, but in space they spread out evenly.

Testing in orbit

Another space advantage is that it is a vacuum – there is no air. Vacuums can be produced on Earth, but it is difficult to make one as "pure" as the real one just outside the walls of a space factory. Some materials are already being tested aboard the ISS and on the Space Shuttle, which has a piece of equipment called the Wake Shield Facility [WSF]. This is able to provide experiments with an even greater vacuum. The results might tell us whether certain materials – for example, the very thin coatings used in computer components – would be better made in space. Such tests will help determine how future space factories will be set up.

In free-fall, crystal growth is faster and produces larger and more consistent structures. These can be used in a wide variety of industries, from medical to computer.

The robotic Shuttle Canadarm lifts the Wake Shield Facility out of the cargo bay. It contains experiments that need to be open to the pure vacuum of space.

A very strange "sci-fi" material – foamed metal. It could be made incredibly strong but light in the microgravity conditions of an orbiting space factory.

Docking ports for the space trucks

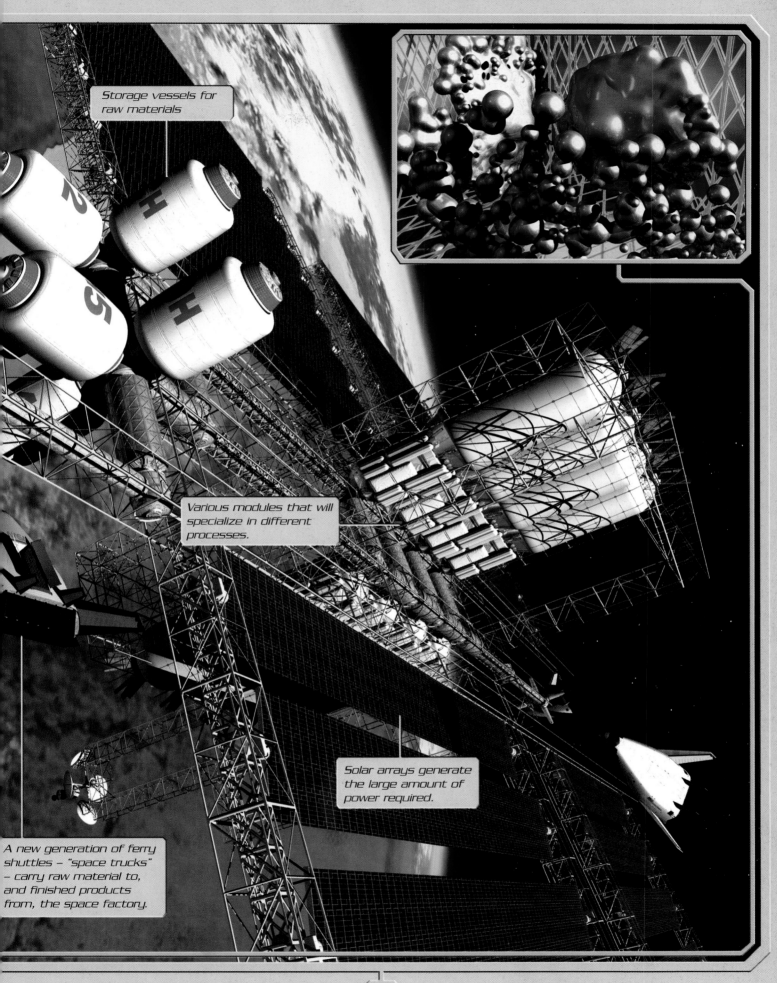

Storage vessels for raw materials

Various modules that will specialize in different processes.

Solar arrays generate the large amount of power required.

A new generation of ferry shuttles – "space trucks" – carry raw material to, and finished products from, the space factory.

POWERHOUSE IN SPACE

Dateline – mid-2000s. This orbiting station is a powerhouse in space. It has huge solar panels that convert energy from the Sun into electricity. This is then used to pump a high-energy laser beam at a cone-shaped spacecraft to produce massive steam power.

Laser light

Laser light is different than the ordinary white light from, say, a flashlight. When a flashlight is turned on, the rays spread out over a wide area and soon lose their power. A laser stays as a tight beam that does not spread, so the energy remains at a high level.

Blasting through space

The laser beam is aimed at a small spacecraft, shaped like a cone. The only fuel on such a cone-ship is a tank of plain water. As the laser hits the base of the cone, so the heat of the beam flash-boils the water into superheated steam. This blasts back from the cone-ship's rear, like a super-power version of the rocket engines of earlier types of spacecraft.

A laser powerhouse makes enough power to beam energy for millions of miles across the gulfs of space. The laser system is very efficient. The Sun provides all energy free, and cone-ships have to carry only water as a fuel. They can reach speeds high enough to cross the Solar System in just a few days.

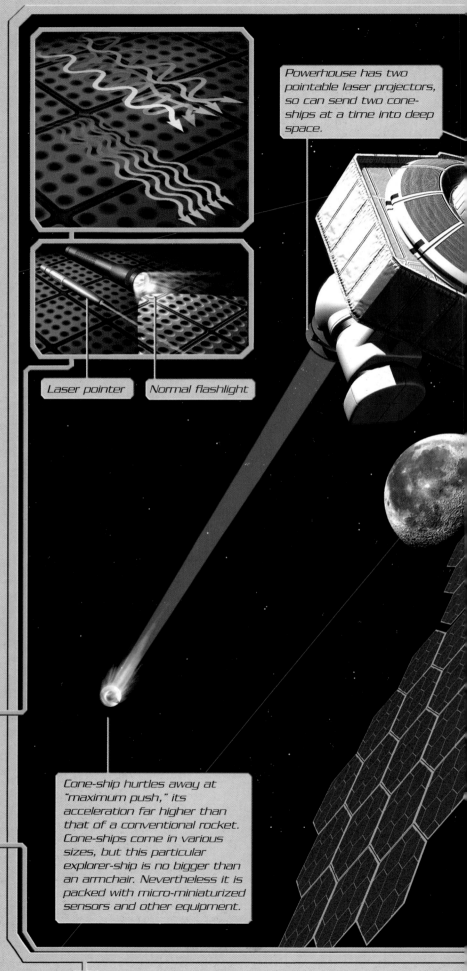

Powerhouse has two pointable laser projectors, so can send two cone-ships at a time into deep space.

Laser pointer

Normal flashlight

An ordinary light beam, made up of many colors of different wavelengths, spreads out and fades away quickly. A laser beam stays in a tight beam of energy.

The cone-ship is a very simple design. A laser beam hits the base and superheats fuel, in this case water. The resulting steam then blasts back to thrust the ship forward at high speed.

Cone-ship hurtles away at "maximum push," its acceleration far higher than that of a conventional rocket. Cone-ships come in various sizes, but this particular explorer-ship is no bigger than an armchair. Nevertheless it is packed with micro-miniaturized sensors and other equipment.

Light beams are shown in all of these diagrams, but light is not normally visible in the vacuum of space.

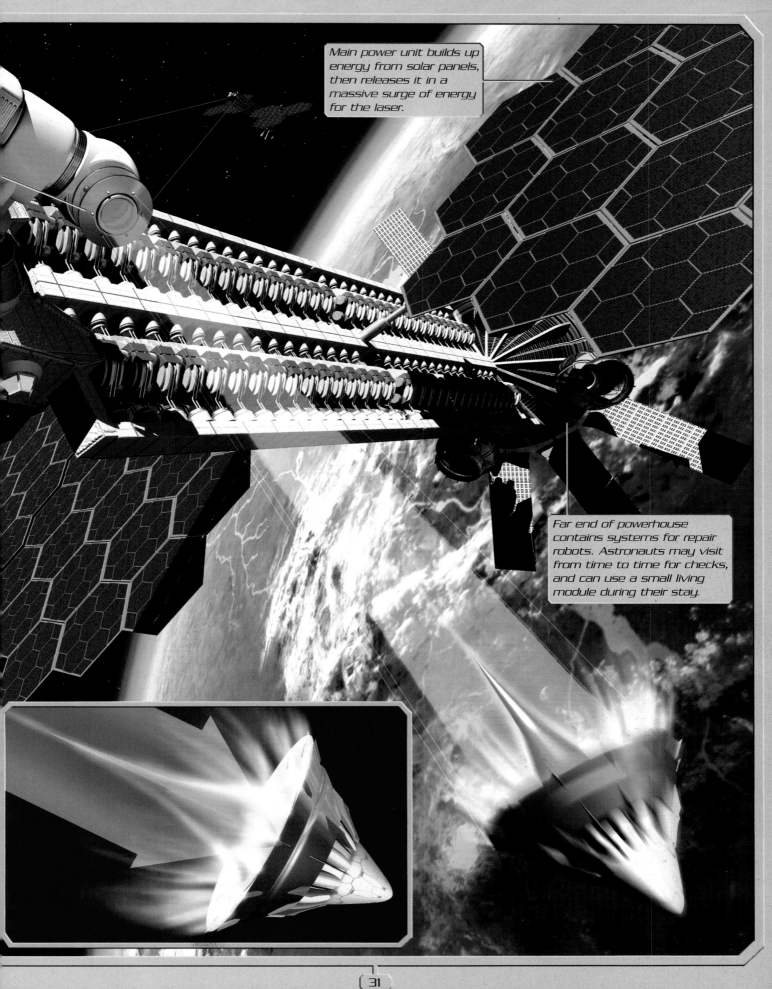

Main power unit builds up energy from solar panels, then releases it in a massive surge of energy for the laser.

Far end of powerhouse contains systems for repair robots. Astronauts may visit from time to time for checks, and can use a small living module during their stay.

HOTEL LUNA

When commercial space travel becomes cheap enough for tourism, it will be time to build the first hotels on the Moon. It's not a far-fetched idea either – the Hilton Hotel group here on Earth has already looked seriously into such a scheme!

A convenient way to start would be to find a suitable crater and build a dome over the top. Here the Moon has a great advantage over building on Earth. Its gravity is only one-sixth that of our planet, so structures can be made larger and less massive. And building materials are on-site, mined directly from lunar surface dust.

When the hotel is open for business, "Moonliners" will bring in visitors from Earth-orbit, landing on special pads nearby. Passengers will then be taken by underground shuttle to the main dome. Once unpacked, visitors staying at the Hotel Luna will find much to see and do. Luxury lunar buses could take you in air-conditioned comfort on journeys across the dusty lunar plains and mountains, visiting sights first seen by astronauts in the 1960s and 1970s.

Interplanetary Olympics

Or maybe tourists will take advantage of the low gravity and try sports unique to the Moon. How about human-powered flight? It should be possible to strap on lightweight wings, and swoop and dive in the hotel's main dome like birds! And a real high spot could be the first Interplanetary Olympics. For Solar System records, adjustments would be made to allow for the low lunar gravity. A lunar high jump would have to be over 48 feet (14.7 m) to beat the present Earth record!

Maintenance plants for waste and air regeneration

Inside the hotel's main dome, the low gravity should be ideal for such sports as human-powered flight.

The main dome sits neatly over a crater. Smaller domes, which connect with the hotel through tunnels, are used for growing food and for staff quarters.

Moonliners land and take off from the three rocket pads.

Communications antenna

Main dome, built over a crater, is tinted to protect tourists from the harsh sunlight.

Lunar tour buses on sightseeing trips – driving over a solar panel by mistake means a heavy fine for the driver!

Solar panels provide power for the hotel.

SPACE-ROCK CITY

Going to the planet Mars is an exciting dream for many people – and one that might be achieved by the middle of this century. But few people think of visiting the tiny moons of Mars – Phobos and Deimos. These minor satellites are potato-shaped chunks of space rock just a few miles long. Yet the larger of the two moons, Phobos, could become an important science base, the headquarters for an exciting project – the "terraforming" of the cold and dry red planet below. Terraforming means creating an Earthlike environment.

Some scientists think that we could do this by redirecting water-ice comets to crash onto Mars to provide some surface water. And seeding the barren soil with genetically modified organisms that can survive in the harsh Martian environment would eventually provide a breathable atmosphere.

Life in a space rock

The Phobos rock-city has comfortable living and working quarters created by drilling machinery. When more room is needed, another tunnel can be drilled. The interior could look much like a shopping mall of today, complete with cafés, bars, oxygen-producing park zones, and other comforts. You would float from place to place in a near-weightless state, because on the tiny world of Phobos you would weigh only a few ounces. The main picture here shows a giant drilling machine, ready to cut into the rock.

A ferry ship emerges from the central core, through a hatch that forms an airtight spacelock. Phobos is not large, but it is big enough to dwarf these spacecraft.

This cutaway view shows how the inside of Phobos can be drilled to make a comfortable rock city. After a few years, the inside might start to resemble a piece of Swiss cheese!

A view down the long central core. It looks a long drop, but in the ultra-low gravity of Phobos you would fall slowly and safely.

Crew in spacepod check the progress of a mining machine.

Giant legs screw into surface to provide grip when drilling starts.

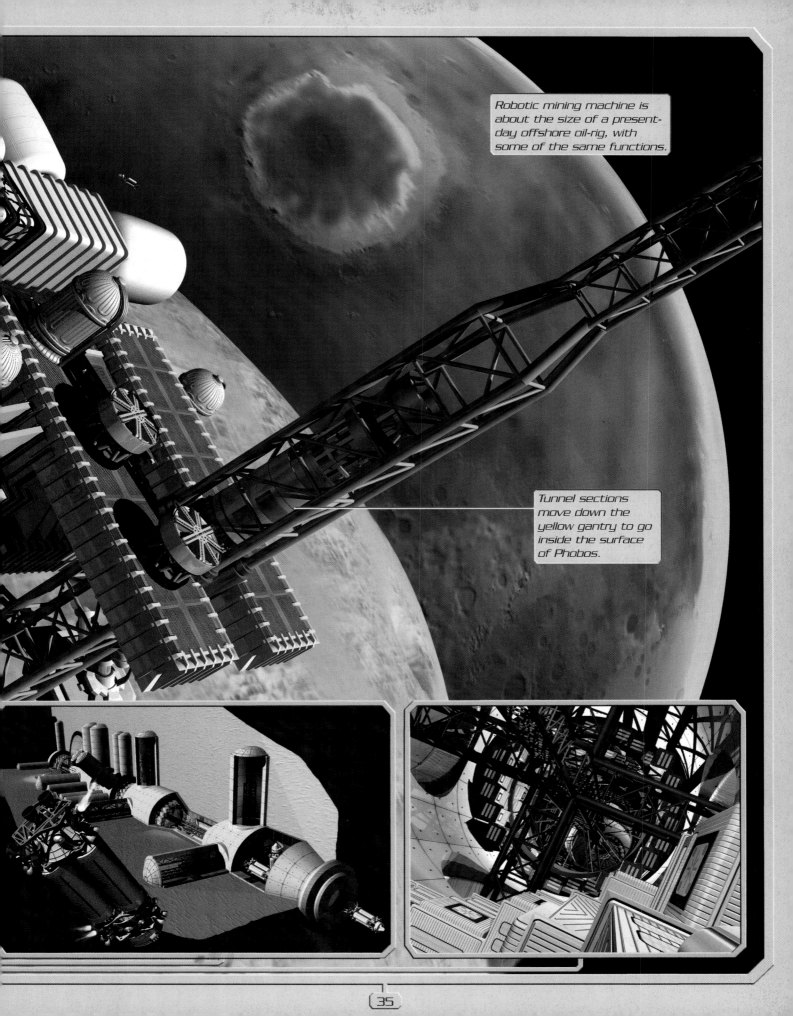

Robotic mining machine is about the size of a present-day offshore oil-rig, with some of the same functions.

Tunnel sections move down the yellow gantry to go inside the surface of Phobos.

CITY ON MARS

Of all planets in the Solar System, the one most like Earth is Mars. So it's a natural target for future colonization. But Mars is not a very welcoming world. Its atmosphere is much thinner than that of Earth, there is no observable surface water, and the temperature sinks far below freezing at night even in the warmest places. It has an ice cap at each pole, but these are composed mainly of solid carbon dioxide.

Our view of Mars has changed over the years. Once it was thought to be inhabited by strange creatures, possibly even intelligent Martians. Then space probes sent in the 1960s and 1970s showed it to be utterly barren, with no signs of life. But since then further robot explorers have shown that conditions are more interesting. There are signs of what look like dried-up river beds. So it seems likely that Mars was once wetter and warmer than it is now. Maybe there was life millions of years ago. Currently there is no proof one way or the other, but studies in 2001 suggest that there may be some underground water near Mars' surface at the present time. Who knows what such discoveries might lead to!

Living on Mars

Mars colonists will live in domes, just as they will on the Moon, and spacesuits will be needed for outdoor exploring. But it may be possible to terraform, or alter the environment on, Mars eventually.

Several probes are due to travel to Mars before 2010, including the British Beagle 2, which will dig under the soil to search for life.

Sojourner rover, the size of a microwave oven, was sent on the Pathfinder probe in 1997. It spent four months exploring near the landing site.

Mars is known as the "red planet" for its overall appearance. It orbits farther from the Sun than Earth does, but its day is only a little longer at 24 hours 37 minutes.

Sky is tinted a pinky-rust color by the airborne dust.

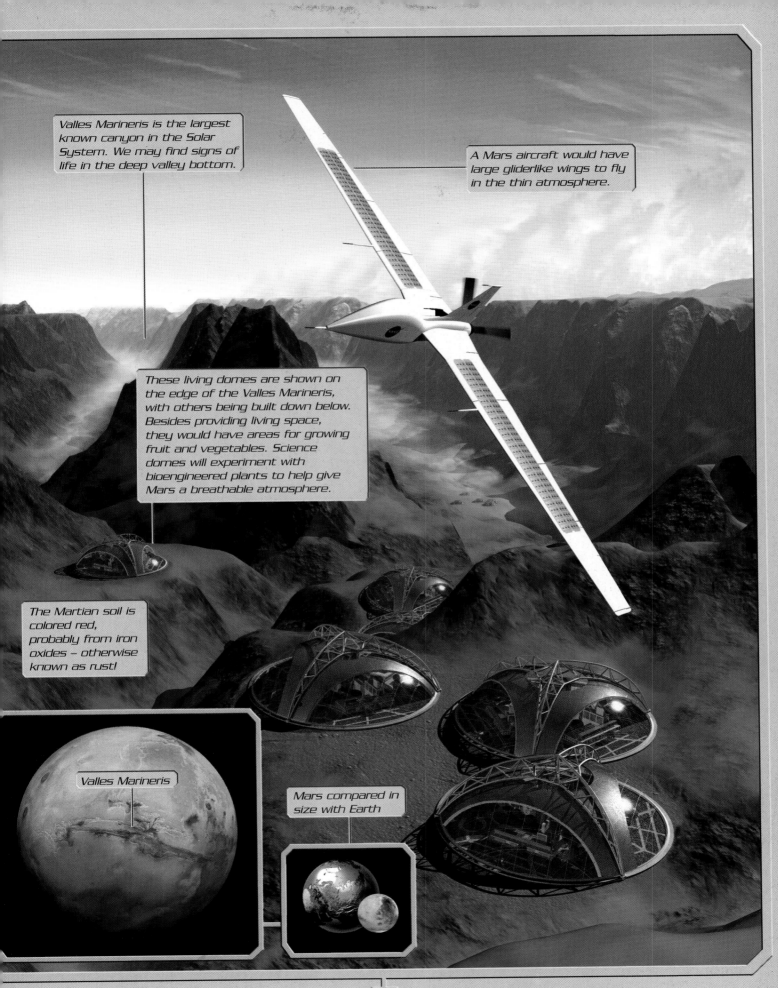

Valles Marineris is the largest known canyon in the Solar System. We may find signs of life in the deep valley bottom.

A Mars aircraft would have large gliderlike wings to fly in the thin atmosphere.

These living domes are shown on the edge of the Valles Marineris, with others being built down below. Besides providing living space, they would have areas for growing fruit and vegetables. Science domes will experiment with bioengineered plants to help give Mars a breathable atmosphere.

The Martian soil is colored red, probably from iron oxides – otherwise known as rust!

Valles Marineris

Mars compared in size with Earth

SPACE COLONY

There are several places in the Earth-Moon space neighborhood called "Lagrange points," after the French scientist who first calculated them in the 1900s. In these areas, gravity forces between Earth and Moon cancel one another out, allowing an object to float in space without drifting away. One such point, L1, is located close to the Moon, on a direct line to the Earth.

The L1 point would be an ideal place to build giant space stations – space colonies – where people could live, work, even raise families. Space colonies might be very large indeed, dwarfing the International Space Station, and could be built using materials from the nearby Moon. But why live in a space colony? There are several reasons to do so. These range from position – the L1 point could be perfect for constructing really big spacecraft – to providing the chance for groups on Earth who might wish to set up independent space communities.

A spinning colony

There is a big difference between the present-day ISS and a future space colony. The ISS floats, but a space colony would rotate slowly to generate artificial gravity at the outer edges. These outer parts would be where people live and work. To enjoy the benefits of free-fall, they could move to the central hub. The colony's spin does not have to be very fast. Generating about one-third Earth's gravity is sufficient to keep people's muscles and bones in good condition.

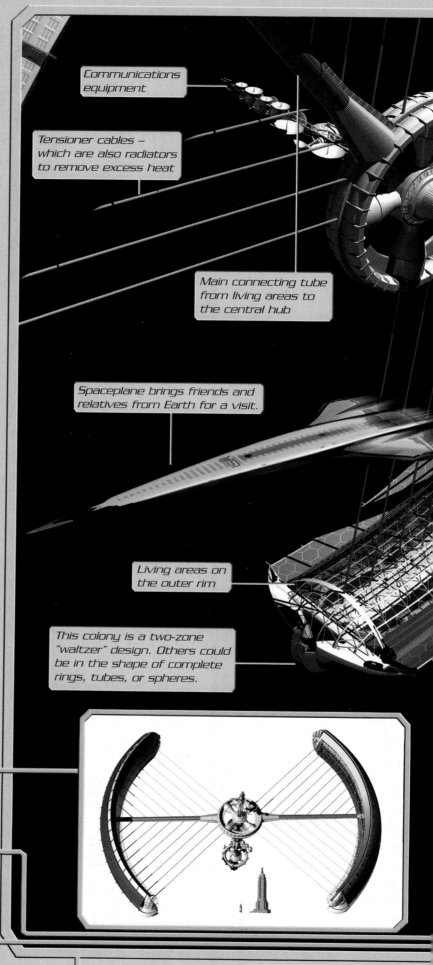

Communications equipment

Tensioner cables – which are also radiators to remove excess heat

Main connecting tube from living areas to the central hub

Spaceplane brings friends and relatives from Earth for a visit.

Living areas on the outer rim

This colony is a two-zone "waltzer" design. Others could be in the shape of complete rings, tubes, or spheres.

A medium-size colony is compared with New York City's Empire State Building and a Space Shuttle.

Work and living areas are on the inside of the rim. Here there could also be trees and grass, maybe even streams and small lakes.

A space colony under construction at L1 is one-tenth of the way from Moon to Earth, giving a magnificent view of our home planet.

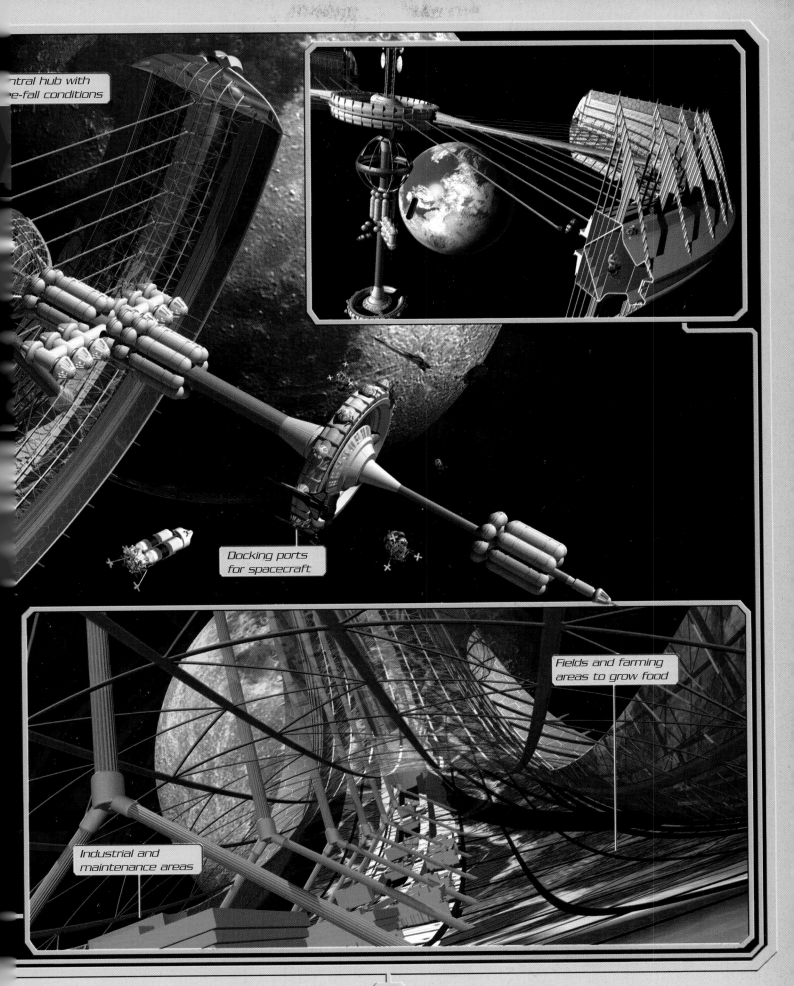

ntral hub with
e-fall conditions

Docking ports
for spacecraft

Fields and farming
areas to grow food

Industrial and
maintenance areas

ORBITAL ELEVATOR

Dateline – mid-2100s. Space elevators are built from Earth's equator to transport people and cargo to and from space easily, quickly, and cheaply.

The person behind this idea was the Russian scientist Yuri Artsutinov. He realized that, if you could lower a cable from a space station to Earth, then you could hoist cargo up and down. using perhaps electric motors, with little more effort than it takes an elevator to go up and down a skyscraper on Earth.

The space station makes one orbit in exactly the same time it takes the Earth to make one rotation, so it would always remain in the same place above the Earth. This can only be done above a point on the equator.

Special materials needed

The materials for building a space elevator need to be super-strong. The elevator runs about 22,300 miles (36,000 km) from Earth, making a huge weight of cable to support.

With high-tech materials. mined perhaps from the Moon or an asteroid. construction of a space elevator would start with a satellite in orbit. The cable would slowly be lowered toward the Earth. Another cable would be sent out in the opposite direction to balance the weight. Once a cable reaches the Earth, the elevator can go to work. Now space launches become cheap and quick. Before long, the elevator will put many conventional rockets out of business.

The elevator's orbital station is a massive city in space. Tourists will use the station as a stop-off point on their way to far-off places, such as the Moon and Mars.

Space elevators are built on the equator, like this one in Kenya, Africa. Other elevators might be built in countries such as Brazil and Indonesia.

At a height of 22,300 miles above the equator, a satellite hovers over one point above the Earth. This is the best place for a space elevator.

Elevator pods

Parking docks for local area spacecraft

Solar panels

Living areas

Hotels and elevator staff living quarters

Parking for ground cars, solar panels on roofs

Earth's equator

Orbital path

Cable to orbit

Elevator orbital station

Here the elevator is shown fixed in Kenya, near Mt Kilimanjaro.

Elevator pods ride up and down the cable.

Solar panels

Huge superlight canopy gives shelter from the Sun.

Terminal areas for trains and buses from nearby airport

ESCAPE FROM THE SUN

Dateline – the far future. The plan – to build a fleet of giant starships, "space arks" that will take people, plants, and animals out of our Solar System to colonize new worlds around other stars.

Building a space ark

Each huge space ark is built in space from materials mined from metal-bearing asteroids. To make the job easier, arks are built in modules, each to a simple design. Robotic workers do the main assembly job, in deep space. When finished, the modules are linked together, and powerful motors are attached to the rear sections.

Snowballs in space

While the space arks are being built, scoop-ships dive into the atmosphere of the giant gas-planet, Jupiter. The ships bring back large quantities of rare gas to fuel the space arks. The frozen fuel – like a giant 12-million-ton "snowball in space" – caps the nose of each space ark. Once the space arks are fueled, loaded, and crewed, these pioneers of the future are ready to set off.

Journey to the stars

Even with a top speed of about 60,000 miles a second (100,000 km/sec), the space arks will take 15-50 years to reach nearby star systems. Each ark starts off with a crew of 200. By journey's end there will be many more people on board, as couples will have families along the way.

These starships are BIG! Here a space ark is compared with the Petronas Towers, Kuala Lumpur, one of the world's tallest buildings, and a large ocean liner. Crew and cargo are carried in linked modules. Fuel forms the huge nose "snowball." Engines are in the tail section. At journey's end, each ship is turned upward and the engines provide braking thrust.

The space ark, more than half a mile (1 km) long, will be built entirely in space. The huge craft is not designed to land on a planet. Shuttles will be used to ferry people to new worlds.

Space ark

Petronas Towers

Ocean liner

Space arks built of space-made materials, far lighter and stronger than possible by Earth factories

Stores module

Engineering module

Living module

Fuel sphere

Nuclear engine module

Sphere is dotted with sensors to monitor fuel state and to check the nearby space environment.

SPACE-TIME ZONE

The first satellite, Sputnik, was sent into space in 1957. After this, the early years of spaceflight saw fantastic progress, and the first men landed on the Moon only eight years after Yuri Gagarin completed the first orbital flight around the Earth in 1961.

Robots instead of humans
But since the last Moon flight mission ended, in 1972, advances in human spaceflight have slowed dramatically, and only robot spacecraft have gone farther than Earth orbit – Space Shuttles and the International Space Station fly just a few hundred miles up. Yet deep-space human spaceflights are not impossible – there were serious plans for Mars spacecraft back in the 1960s. The big problem is finding the money, and few politicians are willing to commit large sums to space adventures.

The high frontier
However, the call of space – the "high frontier" – is as strong as ever, and if ways can be found to make human spaceflight profitable, then the visions in this book could happen. And there are good reasons for traveling to other worlds, apart from the thrill of adventure; we have learned in recent years how fragile our Earth's environment is – so who knows when humans might need to escape to another world.

1957

1ST ARTIFICIAL SATELLITE   Sputnik

1961

1ST MAN IN

2020s-2030s

SPACE TOURS   Spaceplanes and space hotel

2000

INTERNATIO SPACE STAT

2020s-2040s

BATTLE STATION   Space fortress

2030s-2050s

SPACE FACTO

2100s

ESCAPE FROM THE SUN   Space arks

2100s

ORBITAL ELEVATOR   Cable cars to space

2090s-2100s

SPACE COLON

Yuri Gagarin

1969

1ST MAN ON MOON   Historic footprint

1971

1ST SPACE STATION   Salyut 1

First crew take
up residence

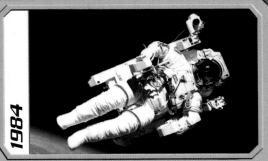

1984

**1ST HUMAN
SATELLITE**   Bruce McCandless
flies MMU

1981

1ST SHUTTLE   Columbia

Making the most
of microgravity

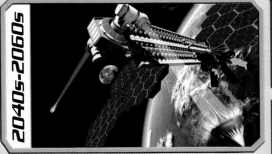

2040s–2060s

**POWERHOUSE
IN SPACE**   Beaming energy
across space

2050s–2100s

HOTEL LUNA   Domed-over Moon crater

Spinning
microplanet

2070s–2100s

CITY ON MARS   Living on the
red planet

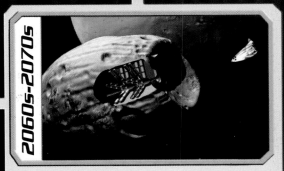

2060s–2070s

SPACE-ROCK CITY   Inside Phobos,
moon of Mars

GLOSSARY

airlock A special module where crews can pass from a spacecraft to space and back. It allows air to be removed when leaving, and to be added on return.

atmosphere The gases that surround a planet. The Earth's atmosphere is made up mainly of the gases nitrogen and oxygen. But other planets have completely different gas mixtures which we cannot breathe.

bioengineering Manipulating living plant or animal cells so that they grow in a particular way.

black hole The remains of an extremely dense star that has "collapsed" in on itself. Nothing – not even light – can escape from a black hole, making its detection very difficult.

Canadarm Canadian-built manipulator arm. One type is used on the Space Shuttle Orbiter. The larger Canadarm2 is used on the ISS.

carbon dioxide A gas found in the atmosphere of many planets.

cargo bay Section of the Space Shuttle that carries satellites, modules, and other equipment into orbit. It is protected during launch and landing by the cargo bay doors.

comet A body, made of ice and dust, that has a very long orbit of the Sun.

cone-ship Design for a spacecraft that would use super-heated steam as fuel for its engine.

crater A circular hole in the surface of a planet or moon made by the impact of something crashing into the ground or by a volcano.

crystal Form of a solid material with naturally flat sides. Sugar and salt grains are familiar examples.

docking The meeting and joining of two spacecraft.

docking port The specific part of a spacecraft used for docking.

exo-planet A planet of a solar system outside our own; short for "extra-Solar planet."

External Tank (ET) Largest single part of the Space Shuttle system. It holds the fuel for the Orbiter's main engines and is normally discarded when empty.

Extra Vehicular Activity (EVA) When an astronaut works outside a spacecraft. Also known as a "space walk."

foamed metal Special form of metal that is honeycombed with gas bubbles.

free-fall The correct term for a "body" – spacecraft or human – in orbit, when it will be weightless (because an orbit is technically a "fall" all the way round a planet); sometimes called "zero gravity" or "zero-G."

global warming The situation where the general temperature of the Earth is increasing. Much global warming is thought to be human-produced, through over-use of certain gases, such as ones contained in some aerosol cans.

gravity The unseen force that keeps us firmly on the Earth. In orbit, gravity is much less, but it is never exactly "zero." The correct term for orbiting craft and crew is that they are in "free-fall" or "microgravity."

ISS The shortened name for the International Space Station. The name "Alpha" may also be used.

Kibo (Hope) Laboratory module of the ISS made in Japan.

Lagrange points Places between Earth and Moon where the gravity forces between these two bodies cancel each other out.

laser A powerful beam of light that does not fan out like a normal flashlight. A laser beam is usually made up of light of one color.

lunar To do with the Moon.

manipulator arm The remotely controlled "robot" arm used to move items around the Space Shuttle and the ISS. Also called a Remote Manipulating System or Canadarm.

Manned Maneuvering Unit (MMU) A one-person backpack, worn by astronauts working around the Space Shuttle and ISS. The MMU is a "mini spacecraft," containing small thruster engines and a life-support system.

meteoroids Bits of space dust and rock particles. When meteoroids reach the Earth's surface they are called "meteorites."

microgravity The tiny gravity pull that is still apparent on board an orbiting craft. On the ISS, microgravity is about one-billionth as strong as on Earth's surface.

Mir (Peace) Russia's most recent space station. It was designed for a five-year mission span, but lasted for 15 years, before reentering the Earth's atmosphere in March 2001.

missile shield General term for protecting a country using space-based weapons to shoot down enemy

missiles. Has also been called "Strategic Defense Initiative" and "Star Wars."

module General name for a piece of space hardware designed to link up with another. One example is the ISS Destiny laboratory module.

Multi Purpose Logistics Module (MPLM) Cylinders used as "moving-trucks" for the ISS. They carry supplies to and from the ISS, traveling in the Shuttle's cargo bay.

orbit The circular or oval path in space that an object takes round another. It applies to the orbit of our Earth round the Sun, as well as to the orbit of a spacecraft round the Earth.

Orbiter Name for the crewed part of the Space Shuttle, but can also be used for any spacecraft that orbits a planet or the Moon.

orbiting height The distance of an orbiting object from the main body; also called its "altitude." This height can vary if the orbit is an oval. For example, the ISS orbits between 220 and 280 miles (350 and 450 km).

ozone One of the gases that surrounds the Earth as the "ozone layer" and which protects us from harmful rays from space. Some scientists think that destruction of the ozone layer may be leading to global warming.

Progress Russian uncrewed supply craft, developed from the crewed Soyuz craft.

rail-gun A type of space weapon that fires solid projectiles, similar to bullets fired by a gun on Earth.

Salyut (Salute) Name for the first Russian space stations. There were seven in total, Salyut 1 being sent into orbit in April 1971.

Saturn Series of U.S. rockets for the Apollo Moon landing programme of the 1960s and 1970s. The Saturn 1B was used for early flights; the bigger Saturn 5 took astronauts to the Moon.

Skylab First U.S. space station, sent into orbit in May 1973. It was converted from the third stage of a Saturn 5 rocket.

solar cells Flat electronic panels that can convert the energy in light to electricity. They are used a great deal in spacecraft as they provide free electrical power by converting light from the Sun.

Solar System Our star, the Sun, and the planets, moons, comets, and other space material that orbit round it.

Soyuz (Union) Russia's crewed spacecraft. The first Soyuz was flown in 1967 and has been updated and improved constantly since. It is also used as the stand-by ISS rescue craft.

space ark A large spaceship that could carry many people to another star system.

space colony A very big space station built as a home for a large group of people.

space probe An unmanned spacecraft sent out to study planets, moons, and other bodies in space.

space station An orbiting spacecraft that is occupied by crews on a permanent, or semi-permanent, basis.

space telescope A telescope used in space. The best known is the HST, or Hubble Space Telescope.

spaceplane General term for a future spacecraft that could take off and land on a runway, like today's airplanes.

spacesuit Special clothing worn by astronauts to protect them from deadly conditions of space. Breathing, heating, and cooling systems are all required.

starship General name for any spacecraft built to travel to other star systems.

superheated steam At ground level on Earth, water boils to form steam at 212°F (100°C). If it is contained under pressure, it boils at a higher temperature and so makes a powerful rocket exhaust.

terraforming Creating an Earthlike environment on another planet or moon.

tether line A strong line that connects an astronaut to a spacecraft during a spacewalk.

vacuum Literally, no air. Most of space is a vacuum, although very tiny electromagnetic particles are always present.

Wake Shield Facility (WSF) Device carried by the Shuttle Orbiter for testing materials in the vacuum of space.

white light Light, as we normally see it, that actually consists of a mixture of all colors. Lasers are usually made up of light of one particular color.

Zarya (Sunrise) The first ISS module to be sent into orbit. It was built in Russia, though commissioned by the U.S. Zarya acts as the control center during the early build-up phases of the ISS.

INDEX